T0065282

SORRY NOT SORRY

*Being grateful, not guilty,
for the good in your life*

ANGELA N. PARRIS

WESTBOW
PRESS®
A DIVISION OF THOMAS NELSON
& ZONDERVAN

Unless otherwise indicated, Bible quotations are taken from the New Living Translation.

WestBow Press books may be ordered through booksellers or by contacting:

WestBow Press
A Division of Thomas Nelson & Zondervan
1663 Liberty Drive
Bloomington, IN 47403
www.westbowpress.com
1 (866) 928-1240

ISBN: 978-1-5127-2266-6 (sc)
ISBN: 978-1-5127-2267-3 (e)

Library of Congress Control Number: 2015920155

Print information available on the last page.

WestBow Press rev. date: 02/03/2016

DEDICATION

This work is dedicated to anyone who's ever felt the cold shoulder of this world or the deprivation of your own mind's foolishness, and still rose above it to share the warmth of God's love with others. Shine baby shine!

CONTENTS

Foreword ix

Acknowledgements xiii

Introduction xv

Chapter 1 – The Power of "I'm Sorry" 1

Chapter 2 – Beautiful Shoes 10

Chapter 3 – One of These Things Is Not Like the Other 19

Chapter 4 – It's Lonely at the Top 27

Chapter 5 – The Penalty (and Pain) of Privilege 36

Chapter 6 – Being Free, Not Defiant 45

Chapter 7 – My Final Apology 51

Chapter 8 – 7 Truths that Stink 54

Afterword 63

Bibliography 65

About the Author 67

FOREWORD

Some time ago, I was waiting in a hotel lobby and noticed a beautiful grand piano in the corner. I took lessons for years and love piano music, so I just stared at the gorgeous Steinway for a while, wishing I had the guts (and remembered enough music) to play it and hear how it sounded. As I was playing like Liberace in my mind, a man sat down and actually started to play. He played Beethoven and he played it beautifully. His hands effortlessly glided over the keys and made the most lovely of sounds. Several people stopped talking and just listened to his music.

When he finished, I went over and complimented him. "Yes, I do think I play rather well," he responded. I was a little taken aback by his candor and when he noticed the look on my face he added, "To deny my ability is to deny the gift that God has given me: a gift for which I am so thankful." What truth in those words! I admired not only his piano playing, but also his honesty, and I wished to be as forthcoming as he.

Sorry Not Sorry is a wonderful book, which explores this tendency in so many of us to apologize for the good in us. Especially we women slouch to mask our height, downplay our accomplishments so that others won't feel bad, hold back so that we don't appear overly assertive. We keep a lid on our personalities and slump our shoulders so that we blend in. I've done this countless times to the point that people thought me insecure and mousy, when really there is a lioness on the inside, wishing I were bold enough and honest enough to let her out!

Scripture says in Psalm 139, *I praise you because I am fearfully and wonderfully made; your works are wonderful, I know that full well* (vs. 14). We are part of God's works, so we are wonderful! You are wonderful! Can you wear that, walk in it, bask in it, and revel in that truth? As Christian women, we read scriptures about the importance of humility and meekness, and some of us have the old fashioned notion that quiet, discrete women get the guy, the job, the promotion and so we wear muted colors, and hold back so that we don't appear proud. But do you know that false humility is another form of pride?

Now, I'm not saying that we should be loud, brash and inappropriate. There are women who live by the motto, "If you've got it, flaunt it!" and so they wear low cut blouses and short skirts, they talk loud and parade through the office demanding attention. I'm not advocating that, and neither is the author. But we are saying, what that pianist in the hotel lobby implied: Be true to yourself and grateful for what you have. If you're tall, walk tall. If you're beautiful, be grateful for your looks, not apologetic. If you're smart, don't dumb down to appear average. If you're talented, let's see it! But get this: we don't do this to draw attention to ourselves, but ultimately to draw attention to God. I love it when Christian athletes score and then while the crowd is going crazy, they point upwards to God, implying that it was God who gave them the ability to make that shot. They are transferring the praise through themselves back to Him. Note, they do not hold back and fail to take the shot for fear of looking good. They boldly take the shot but when they score, they give the glory to God. That's what we should do in everything, all the time.

As the author writes so well, "Glorify God with your gifts and use your advantage for good; your life and the world around you will be better for it."

In order for us to glorify God with our gifts, we first have to acknowledge them to be gifts and then use them for good. How many of us have hidden our abilities under a bushel, instead of letting them shine for all to see? Remember the parable of the talents (Matthew 25:14-30)? It was the servant who hid his talent out of fear (fear of making a mistake, fear of what others would think, fear of whatever!) that received the master's wrath. The ones who responded in gratitude and used their talents received praise and were given more.

Saints, as Mrs. Parris so rightly says, "We are at our best when we confidently operate in our gifts and blessings." Amen! Don't hold back. Walk in it, give God the praise for it and He will give you even more.

In closing, I will tell one last story. I grew up in Brooklyn, went to public schools and then had the fortune of getting accepted to Dartmouth College. This was a big deal for my family. I didn't come from a long line of Ivy Leaguers. There were no trust funds or plaques with our family name on it. I came from a working class, mixed race family and I happened to do well in school. I wasn't a brain and my IQ score is not impressive, but I did get a lot of A's in high school, I played the piano *and* I did miraculously go to Dartmouth. I used to say to people, "I went to college in New Hampshire." I wouldn't necessarily share the Dartmouth part because I didn't want to appear snooty or arrogant. I wanted to blend in and just be regular. But God convicted me one day that I was denying Him the glory that is due Him. I know that it was God's grace that got me in and kept me in until graduation day. He is the author of any intelligence I have. He moved the pieces, gave me favor and willed for me to go there. Not me. And so now when people ask where I went to school, I say it like it is, "I went to Dartmouth and I'm so grateful for that experience." That is the honest truth. If people want to think I'm a snob, that's their problem.

Sisters and brothers, don't be sorry for what God has given you. Walk in humility knowing that true humility is acknowledging God's goodness in your life and allowing Him to use it for His purposes.

Nicole Doyley
Author of *The Wait: Encouragement for Single Women*

ACKNOWLEDGEMENTS

I serve the most amazing God! Thank You for redeeming me and for kindling a fire in me that no darkness will ever consume. I married the most amazing man – I Cor. 13 all day baby! I have the most amazing family and friends! Thanks for riding the front seat of this spine-tingling rollercoaster with me – You're my heroes. I had the most incredible childhood! Thanks mom and Tara for never bursting my bubble – what welfare?! I've lived amongst the most caring communities. Thanks from the East to the West Coasts, for showing me that having God's blessing doesn't exempt us from needing His grace. God bless you Jeff C. for Gladys and Buber – you are ministry in motion, and to Patty L. for calm and steady support in the timeliest of seasons – you are a rock.

INTRODUCTION

I'm walking in authority
Living life without apology
It's not wrong dear
I belong here
So you might as well get used to me
Written by Donnie McClurkin: Don Mac Music &
Seven Summits Music (2003)

While contemplating God's splendor, David lifted praises to God because He created mankind with such marvelous efficacy. You were created by a divine God who, in His infinite wisdom, took great care to put you together specifically for the life that was planned for you long before you were born. (Psalm 149:13 & 139:13) Try to really embrace what that means about your life. Though you might feel like it sometimes, you are not some insignificant speck on the face of a random cosmic kingdom. There wasn't a blueprint created for you – you are the blueprint. And because He created you in His own image and placed His nature inside of you, there are dreams, aspirations, questions and longings that will only be fulfilled in the wisdom of the very same God who made you. Your standard is not accurately measured in the societal doctrines that have surrounded you since birth; you will never be satisfied with those expectations. Instead, the standard for your life is determined by one thing and that alone – your faith in your Creator to follow the path that He designed just for you. (2 Cor. 10:12-16) Sure there are flaws and shortcomings in your nature, but this book doesn't focus on those as much as the gifts and greatness that are within each of us to perform the Will of God for our lives. There will be plenty of times where the flaws are pointed out. But here's the real deal. You are not a mistake or some unlucky coincidence. It's time now, to put your ingenuity and magnitude on display and there will be no apologies made for it. After all, your assets - your favor - come from God.

Apologetics is a term which describes the discipline of defending one's position on an idea or set of ideas and is most commonly associated with religion. Scholars, theologians and sociologists have employed this method of argument to influence others with respect to their particular position on an issue, typically related to religion. The irony surrounding this aged practice, is that Christianity emboldens the worldview that faith in Christ does not require a defense. Apologetics on the other hand, have galvanized this practice in light of its reliance on evidence and historicism. Perhaps it has something to do with writings such as 1 Pet 3:15 that let us know believers are to be ready at all times to give an answer for their hope in Christ. It's important not to assign human reasoning to a divine text. Peter was providing strategies for Christians who were being persecuted for doing what was right by God. In this way, it becomes easy for goodhearted people to behave erroneously because we may not grasp the principle behind the practice. Anyone who endeavors to live Holy, but attempts to do so through natural methods, will always fall short of the mark at which they are aimed. The Apostle Paul masterfully conveyed the perfect balance of recognizing our human shortcomings, while also valuing our divine opportunities:

> "I don't mean to say that I have already achieved these
> things or that I have already reached perfection. But
> I press on to possess that perfection for which Christ
> Jesus first possessed me." (Philippians 3:12)

Among these pages, you may discover that this same well-intentioned yet erroneous practice has found its way into your life. This is not an assault on Apologetics as a discipline. Rather, it is an attack on the enemy who has subtly crept into the thinking of many believers and convinced us that we should shun success, greatness and other blessings which God chooses to place in our path. Marianne Williamson puts it this way, "Our deepest fear is not inadequacy but that we are powerful beyond measure." In her 1992 publication *A Return to Love* © *Harper Collins Publishers* she admonishes us:

You are a child of God
Your playing small does not serve the world.
There is nothing enlightened about shrinking
so that other people won't feel insecure around you.
We are all meant to shine, as children do.
We were born to make manifest the glory of God that is within us.
It's not just in some of us, it is in everyone.

CHAPTER 1

THE POWER OF "I'M SORRY"

I'm Sorry. These tiny little words have immense power between them. Still they are often underestimated and imperfectly deployed. When spoken, they can bring comfort and restoration to a broken heart. Withheld, they can prolong pain and increase suffering with reckless abandon. As with any power, the effect of "I'm sorry" impacts both the giver and the receiver. Haven't you been there? Desiring the apology of someone who has hurt or wrongfully accused you. Maybe you've been on the other side, extending an apology and being able to feel the air break as tension dissolves and you realize restoration is beginning. Whichever side of an apology you've experienced, there's no doubt that it has the power to build up or to tear down.

So what is an apology? Or rather, what is its nature and power? An apology, much like a baptism or Christening, is an outward expression of something that has taken place on the inside of a person. It formally acknowledges that you need another's love, forgiveness, or grace. An apology recognizes that a breach has been made in a relationship, that someone doesn't want that

1

breach to continue, and so it attempts to reconcile that breach. (J. Clark)

Most people would agree that any time one person hurts another, an apology should be offered IF the offender wishes to maintain the relationship. Many would also agree that the apology should be sincere and not forced. All things considered, when something goes wrong between two people, an apology is a good place to start in order to get things back on track. But what about when your apology isn't about something you've done but instead something you are? If you're rich and it makes people around you uncomfortable, is the apology still warranted? What if you're always getting A's on tests or you're the high scorer in every athletic competition you enter? Is an apology still warranted? Should a Pastor of a congregation in the thousands, feel sorry for the Pastor over 25 or 50 members? For several years I wondered about questions like this but not enough to do something about it. I didn't think it had anything to do with me. Still, I couldn't point to any specific evidence that it was wrong, but I felt strongly that no one should have to apologize for the favor God has bestowed upon them. Eventually God showed me just how much this line of questioning had to do with me. I was about to embark on a journey of self-discovery. I was about to see how I had been apologizing for my own identity... not just once but as a result of two significant seasons of my life – first my natural birth and then again in my new birth with Christ.

I had been living out "I'm Sorry" for years without realizing it. Even so, my apologetic thinking was self-inflicted and erroneous. It had crept in and disguised itself as unpretentiousness and even modesty. This "I'm Sorry" had grown up with me and matured in its expression through my young adult years until the moment it arrested the very core of my being. In my mind, I began to replay various times when I held back some piece of myself more than I should have because I was trying to be humble. Humility isn't something you put on and take off; it becomes you and you become it as you mature spiritually. After all humility is a by-product of the Fruit of The Spirit so its nature is divine. (Gal 5:22) I began to realize that I had formed a faithful habit of appearing to be less than I was, because I was so anxious about not making others uncomfortable with me. I had manufactured my own brand of humility and meekness. I'm not proud of it, but admitting to what's in the mirror is the first step to correcting it.

> *humility is a by-product of the Fruit of The Spirit so its nature is divine.*

I subscribe to the belief that God is the Creator of all things and that He admires His creation. That means you and me. Somehow that statement is easier to think about than to act upon. How had I become so broken and concerned with what other people thought to the point where I was remorseful about the talents, favor and blessings that God saw fit to place in my life? It was hard to embrace, but I realized that we can't add any value to another person's life by diminishing the value of our own.

> "You are the light of the world – like a city on a hilltop that cannot be hidden. No one lights a lamp and then puts it under a basket. Instead, a lamp is placed on a stand, where it gives light to everyone in the house. In the same way, let your good deeds shine out for all to see, so that everyone will praise your heavenly Father." (Matt 5:14-16)

As a child, I developed a limitless alter-reality for myself. I was convinced that anything that could happen in my head, could happen in reality. This mindset followed me into adolescence but played out in more of a subconscious way. The benefit of thinking this way, was that it helped to shape me into becoming a very resourceful person. If I could conceive it, I could achieve it; I only needed to figure out *how* and anything became possible. I mean I really drank the Kool-Aid on this one! Still, at some point in my life that philosophy lost its credence.

I began placing limits on myself and identifying obstacles to achieving those dreams. As I reflected back over the seasons of my diminishing confidence, I realized a pattern. I would be in a winning state – a consistent pattern of abundance or gain – and just when I thought someone else might not like it, I'd back down. I was promoted quickly in professional and religious settings and I had a natural tendency to move confidently in the gifts and skills that I brought to those settings. Still, I developed a keen awareness to the shifts in people's body language if I was getting "too much shine". I would quickly modify my performance to try and be less noticeable just to try and avoid the discomfort that would often follow.

There is one conversation I will never forget. A former colleague asked me to lunch because she was considering a career move and wanted to hear my thoughts on her considerations. We were enjoying our meal at a sidewalk café while discussing some of the jobs she might explore. At some point, she made a statement that went far beyond my ears and struck a chord in my soul. I could barely remember every word but it went something like, "blah blah blah, and *like you* I wasn't confident about my skills… blah blah" I replayed those words in my head as she continued to talk. Then suddenly the sounds of passing traffic and dishes clanking on tables and the mindless chatter of patrons all around us seemed to amplify by about 1000 times! Could she hear that too?! Why was she still talking? My ears began to throb as I remembered other conversations with professionals who poured out my accolades but not without sliding in the occasional remark about how they could relate to my 'lack of confidence'. She continued to go on and I continued to play the confidence remarks that had shattered my attention on anything in that present moment. "Who wasn't confident?" I thought to myself. Hadn't I always been poised and secure in my dealings with other professionals? After all, I worked super hard at proving myself because I was usually the youngest amongst my colleagues. I was usually the only minority among my colleagues (or on the floor or in the whole division quite honestly) and I was always the least tenured. These challenges shaped me into a super congenial, above-and-beyond machine of efficiency who was always open to becoming better. My confidence about my job performance was substantiated by the reviews and promotions I had received. Even so, my actions didn't seem to convey that confidence. I had become consumed with convincing others that I was a team player - no better and no less than them. And then it hit me! All of that cowering down and trying to be humble wasn't coming off as modesty. They thought I was insecure! I could only imagine how many other promotions I had averted because of my 'modesty'.

I quickly realized that I had created a mess only God Himself could straighten out. The awful truth about my fabricated version of humility, was that it didn't have the power and sincerity of divine humility. This was all me; and worse – it eventually began to work against me. Divine humility works in our favor because it comes from God and his wisdom is infinite. Our wisdom is limited! I could've saved myself a lot of grief, though I don't regret not understanding that better at the time. In that season, God had an encourager in position for me. My husband regularly showered me with compliments and often told me how invaluable my skills were for the jobs or groups in which I had been placed. He would tell me how necessary it was for me to continue to be myself even though it seemed like whenever I did, someone would have a problem with it. Still, he pushed me and affirmed me and I eventually came to understand that it was easier to just do things the way I did them. Trying to be something I wasn't, was way more work than it was worth – even if I thought I was doing it out of consideration for others. God comforted me through my husband, just as He does for many of us through some person in our lives whose words we don't receive earnestly enough at the time. Though it took me some time to learn how to just say, "thank you" I found liberty in being able to do so. After a while, I said it and meant it. That meant I believed and agreed with the compliment that was shared towards me.

- Do you find yourself 'dialing back' your personality, skills or accomplishments because you believe you will 'blend' better?
- Has God has placed someone in your life who occasionally affirms you or validates your personality, skills or accomplishments?

If so, try to tune in to what is being said and learn to appreciate the sincerity behind the words. Gratitude conquers all types of fear. Say thank you and start to believe again, and you may even start to see yourself the way they see you. God loves us so much! True recognition of this fact compels the believer to love Him that much more, because He first loved us. (I John 4:19)

In fact, 'thank you' became the two words that replaced 'I'm sorry' in my innermost thoughts and subconscious behaviors. I never actually said the words, "I'm Sorry" for being gifted or skilled at something. I didn't spew off actual apologies when I thought my presence made someone else uncomfortable. I did, however, *behave* like I was sorry by trying to fall back or otherwise blend in. Each time I shied away from a compliment or an opportunity to face a challenge I was saying, "I'm sorry God that you meant this for me, but You must not have known I couldn't do it" and I would hold back. Contrition had replaced my gratitude for the greatness God placed within me. The "I'm Sorry" that I lived with all of those years, had arrested my development, held up progress of groups and companies where I served, and it kept me from fully experiencing the unimaginable blessings that I dreamt about in my youth. Oh to be young and free from the apprehensions of an adult mind!

Children rarely share the considerations that adults have when it comes to world views. I remember as a child, the moment it really sunk in, that not everyone spoke the same language as me. I had to be in first or second grade. It fascinated me so. But it wasn't until fourth or fifth grade when I walked home past a classmate's house, that this notion really took hold of me. He was Vietnamese and his mother spoke to him in their native language at the door, beckoning him to hurry home to get started on his homework. I recall how incessant she seemed, waving wildly with her hands as if he shouldn't've been walking with the other kids and me. Still, until then my ears hadn't been so captivated by the exclusivity that belonged to them because only Phong and his mother, perhaps anyone else in the house, understood what she was actually saying... and I wanted in. That very day, I decided I wanted to speak another language. Only I didn't think it was necessary to learn one formally. Instantly, I began babbling and emulating sounds and utterances that sounded to me, just like what I heard at Phong's doorstep and in my friend Carlos and Ilia's house. Somewhere between Spanish and an Asian dialect I wouldn't even be able to appreciate until much later in life, I began speaking another language. I would ramble it off to myself, my friends in school and all the time around the house. I couldn't understand for the life of me why no one ever understood what I was saying! One day someone, I don't remember who, asked me to stop all that babble and speak "right". Had I been speaking "wrong" all that time? Did I say a bad word? After multiple requests over time to 'cut it out' I began to yield and my bubble was burst. I was forced to accept that the murmurings and tongue-tingling chatter I had come to love and share with confidence, may have been offensive to someone who identified with a particular ethnicity or culture. The real disappointment however, was realizing that what had meant so much to me, didn't have nearly the same value to others around me. I stopped speaking my new 'tongue' - out loud anyway. And soon after, my love for lingo was squelched. I had given up something I loved and devoted myself to, because others didn't seem to regard it as I had. Eventually, I let it go. By the way, the same

7

thing is known to have happened concerning the divine speaking in tongues or other spiritual gifts.

Have you ever met someone who is small in physical stature, but has a great big presence or personality? Someone who perhaps believed they were just like other big people, until someone burst their bubble and made them believe they were small. It's heart-wrenching to witness, even destructive when you realize that it's happening to you. Funny how God will allow the aspirations of your younger days, to stay with you and resurface at different points in life as you evolve. It's like He knew what He was doing when He made you with them. I eventually studied French. I learned a lot of Spanish from my environment and I even took courses in American Sign Language. Today I still have a fascination for words – the way they sound with various accents, how they roll from the tongue and require certain lip and tongue posture – the variation of meaning within a word. Well, I just really love words and language. It seems though, that we sometimes give up before the polishing process is complete. What's the polishing process? This occurs during the development of some spiritual character and comes right after the fieriest season of that development. You've been shaped and molded, but you're still not quite your best. In this process, the making has already occurred so you know what you are; but a polishing enhances and distinguishes you so that others will see your upgrade in its true light. Giving up before this process occurs may cause you to see something amazing inside of yourself, but the view might be limited to just you. In speaking other languages, trying new things, venturing into the deep places of a faith-filled life, we must hang onto love and faith during the polishing process and in this way we will find good favor with God and man. (Prov. 3:1-4) I started learning those languages as an adult – really learning them – and I've been able to help others in doing so. Once I told God (and meant it) just how sorry I was for getting mad and cutting out before time, I was ready to be fully restored and set back on the path of possible impossibilities. You can too. And if it starts with a mutter no one else likes, don't be sorry, be grateful!

Say this prayer aloud: *"Lord, forgive me for not seeing myself as you see me. I place my gifts and callings back in your hands, and I am committed to being your living epistle here on Earth – sometimes the only church people will see. Help me to remember that it's not me others see when I shine, but You. In that truth I am permitted to excel in every good work done on Your behalf."* Amen

CHAPTER 2

BEAUTIFUL SHOES

For all of my life I've looked up to my big sister – still do. We didn't have any other siblings and although my sister had hoped I would be a boy, my mother brought home a bouncing baby girl complete with an inner-cheerleader and a healthy Barbie-hankering. Needless to say, my sister wasn't exactly stoked, but she loved me still. We didn't look very much alike. People would sometimes comment on how different we looked from one another. They would dismissively talk about how "I had good hair but my sister did not." Family members and classmates would carelessly ramble off remarks because our skin color was different, our hair texture was different, or our shapes and sizes were different. She played basketball and I was a cheerleader. She got C's in school and I got A's. I was having Madonna dress-up parties in my room with the door open while my sister ripped off Queen Latifah or Run DMC lyrics with her door shut. As we grew, I came to hate the disrespectful way that people would compare us because it always seemed to pit us against one another. Funny thing is I never ever saw her the way that people depicted. I was angry with the others, but I never ever thought my sister would be genuinely angry with me because of it. This was how God made us and we shouldn't feel like it was our fault – or anyone's fault for that matter. I wasn't sorry about it.

The more things change, the more they stay the same. When I was a child, I remember thinking that people were a little too comfortable saying whatever came to their mind regarding the appearance or lifestyle of another person. As if it was okay not to regard the feelings of the person they were talking about, an adult might say, "What a strange-looking child... so dark-skinned". Some kid on the playground would disrespectfully talk about the ugly clothes of another child. Then someone else would go a step further and compare the youth to his better-looking brother or sister. I call it "The Talk" mostly because to me it seems to be the thoughtless chatter of a person who makes no consideration for the consequences of his words. For the most part I was usually on the kinder end of The Talk for a lot of my life. At least when people talked about me in my presence. They would complement my pretty hair or talk about my cute cheeks, nice clothes or slender figure after having given birth to six children. You'd think I would be grateful for that, but I often found myself distraught by it because I would be thinking about the hurt of others who weren't getting similar compliments. I had friends and loved ones who were often on the hurtful end of The Talk and I didn't want to be separated from them in that way. After all, my friends and family were always as attractive to me, as I was to The Talkers and I couldn't understand how they didn't see it. This would anger me because of the affect that outsiders could have on the relationships around me. The Talk has the ability to drive a stake of dissention right through a friendship; it severs bonds which have nothing to do with the inside of a person – the only character that really matters. Have you ever witnessed the Talk? Which side of the remarks have you been on?

My sister was always attractive to me. Her style, those perfect teeth and that voice! Yes, I saw our differences quite unlike the views of some thoughtless people around us. Over the years, I continued to neglect giving attention to how The Talk might've impacted my sister until one evening when I was sitting on the floor of her closet admiring the sea of beautiful shoes lined up like a Beverly Hills showroom. As I strolled slowly along the wall of footwear making sure to paw each one as if it were a Lenox original, I asked her why she had so many beautiful shoes, clothes and purses when she couldn't possibly enjoy wearing them all. She didn't answer right away but after a bit more chatter she responded, "I do it now, because I couldn't pull it off then - in childhood". She continued, "You were the girlie one and I was too fat to pull off that style." My heart dropped. I could barely catch my breath and I didn't know what to say. I don't believe I said anything, worthwhile anyway. My sister is a buxom beauty, complete with a full figure, golden skin and teeth like the pearly gates of Heaven. It had taken more than 30 years for me to learn that she didn't feel beautiful or feminine in her youth. As a result, she tried to make up for lost childhood by dressing up her outer appearance as an adult. She pulled out another beautiful shoe – this time it was a shimmery glass-like stiletto with straps so fragile they looked as if they would pop if you tied them too tightly.

We continued our discussion. My mom had joined us on the floor by now. I remember saying something about not really caring too much about whether people thought I was pretty. All the while I was secretly questioning whether that was true. My sister flinched as she pulled the shoe strap over her heel. Maybe I did care, but not because I was worried they didn't like me. Maybe I cared because I thought they'd think my sister wasn't pretty enough. Had I actually become consumed with this to the point that I took action into my own hands? By now, she was writhing around the floor grabbing her calve and moaning in pain. "Why don't you just take it off?" I remember asking her. She shot a look at me and continued talking while I drifted between that moment and our childhood. I remembered the little ways I used to intentionally prevent any focus on me by highlighting her best features before anyone had a chance to compare us. There were times that I would not go places she was hanging out just so that she wouldn't have the disruption of a "pretty" little sister around. And I think I missed some good parties too! That arresting moment on the floor of my big sister's closet, where I still looked up to her in so many new ways, was the start of my journey to reflect on the role I may have played in this cruel childhood experience. What I discovered next would shape my perspective on God's blessings in a way I had never imagined. There are people in this world who will behave crudely; they may say harsh words or treat you in an unpleasant manner. The reasons won't always be known or even make sense at times. But as quickly as I realized how those experiences shaped my sister's behaviors, I also realized that my behavior was no better. And right there on that floor God showed me how it wasn't just my sister who needed to change on the inside, but also me.

Children don't always recover so quickly from experiences like this. Before long, I had subconsciously programmed myself to 'dim down' my own light whenever I wanted people to see my sister positively. I wanted so badly for others to see her the way that I saw her so I did whatever I could to, well... disappear. I felt like that was the only power I had to make sure I wasn't the reason she didn't get the attention that I felt she deserved. How arrogant of me. I began to think about other people in my life and other circumstances when I felt I

> *I had subconsciously programmed myself to 'dim down' my own light*

was being distinguished, where I would intentionally pretend to be less impressive so they could feel appreciated. Little did I realize this had become a lifelong pattern that would ultimately hinder the gifts that God had given me to use for His glory. I had become sorry for being made pretty. I began to welcome criticism and I even offered my own self-condemnation if no one else did. You know, not taking a compliment without offering a defense. "Your hair is so pretty." "Thanks but you didn't see how much I had to fight to get it to look like this." Responding to admiration by pointing out my flaws. "You look great for having six kids!" "Thanks but everybody has their scars…here, look at these varicose veins!" When I realized that I had become so apologetic I was shocked and ashamed. And all of this was going on in my head without my sister ever knowing, or probably caring. After all, she had just revealed a longtime pain and coping mechanism of her own. And there I was trying to get a grip on my own epiphany without looking like I had just peed on myself. The humiliation of that moment was so unbearable that I still don't remember the words and events that followed that conversation for the remainder of my visit.

Later that week when I returned home I had a serious heart-to-heart with God. It went something like this:

> *Ok God (this wasn't one of those "Dear God" moments), so it wasn't my fault that people were so ignorant towards my sister, and therefore towards me. Why then, did their words have such a lasting impact on her life? And God responded, "Your questions are about [your sister] but I want you to look in your own mirror and ask what impact it had on you".* The nerve of God. I immediately left the conversation feeling somewhat angry, but mostly confused that He managed to turn this around on me. I found myself back at His feet a few days later – only this time I was in my place as his child. *"Daddy, if I only consider my own experience, isn't that being selfish since my sister took on most of the wounds from this?"* And He didn't respond immediately, leaving me with my own voice and thoughts to process. A few days more and a small, still voice stirred a chill in me that brought on endless tears for months to come – *"Do you not see where you have abandoned your ambitions, cut down your dreams… my dreams for you, and behind this mask of what you*

call humility, you have tried to convince yourself and others that what I have put in you, is too much for them to handle?" I was rendered motionless. The room seemed to go even darker than it was and if an ant moved, I would've felt it only I couldn't tear my attention away from what I was beginning to hear in the Spirit. *"You child, are the one who is overcompensating for something that happened, but over which you have no control…and no authority".* I was done.

For as long as I can remember, I was a confident person. To think of all the people who had been in my life who were fighting self-esteem issues or identity crises! The many times I found myself in disbelief that a person couldn't see her own outer beauty because her skin was dark or her eyes were small or her hair wasn't very long, and God compelled me to encourage and reassure them of their beauty. Who would've thought that one day I would come face to face with my own insecurity over being seen as pretty by anyone? If you have hated on pretty people, you're not likely going to connect with this right away but read on and look for the similarities of any pain that comes from a false sense of identity. If it meant that someone else was going to be demeaned, I didn't want any part of it. So by my own actions I had become programmed to self-destruct.

> "Because of the privilege and authority God has given me, I give each of you this warning: Don't think you are better than you really are. Be honest in your evaluation of yourselves, measuring yourselves by the faith God has given us. (Rom 12:3)

Verses like this had been firmly implanted in my head; only I had applied them far beyond the context which God intended. But the key to really embracing that instruction was in the second sentence. We are to evaluate ourselves, not by our human traits but instead by our faith in God. Whoa! I had been evaluating myself incorrectly for as long as I could remember. It's bad enough trying to measure up to someone else, but even measuring yourself to yourself will produce an incorrect assessment of your worth. Now that I could finally receive God's perspective on this, He could begin to de-program the incorrect thinking and behaviors that had become so much a part of my life.

This was no overnight process. In the months that followed that night in my sister's closet, I began to place every thought and interaction under a microscope to this new understanding. Not exactly what God needed me to do, but at least I didn't abandon the revelation altogether. And it finally paid off. One Friday night while I was in prayer at church, I found myself lying prostrate on the altar and crying out to God asking Him to forgive me for being sorry about how He made me. I poured out my heart about what I had discovered I was doing. I argued with God about how I thought it was right to make sure others felt more important than I was. I cried and fussed and blubbered until I could hardly stay awake. And just as I had resigned in my heart that I would be stuck in this realization forever and that I wasn't worthy of moving past this erroneous lifestyle that I had created in the wondrous name of Our Lord, God spoke to me in an audible voice, "I am perfectly pleased with what I have made; now get up and stop apologizing for me – I am not sorry". By now the scheduled prayer time was long over and everyone else had already taken their seats. Any other time I might've been embarrassed to be moving out of the order of service, but in this particular moment there was a peace within me that didn't allow for embarrassment. I was fearfully and wonderfully made and that was no mistake. Flaws and all, God was pleased with His creation – me – and nothing would give me the right again to be displeased.

Just like Jeremiah, God the Creator of both my sister and me had taken great care to knit us together and bring two very distinctly beautiful people into the world through the same extraordinary mother. A little light was placed within each of us as a tool to bring light to dark places in the world – different places for my sister than for me. The light was given to each of us and was not meant to be smoldered because of others' discomfort. In fact, it's for others' sake that our lights must shine brightly. I had to learn that my light shining would never mean my sister's light wouldn't shine in its own glory; if people were unable to see her light, it was more likely about the condition of their blindness and not about something that I or she, had done. In short – her light had nothing to do with me. My perspective had, embedded deep within it, a version of pride that is at the very core of the sin cycle. If I was honest with myself, I had been acting as if God messed up and I was trying to cover for His mistake by making myself over every time this experience would arise.

- Have you ever known that God is calling you to do something, but stalled because of what you believed others might think?
- When others compliment you, do you respond with self-criticism or critique?
- Do you sometimes feel like someone near to you would be better off if people didn't compare him/her to you?

If you see yourself in any of these questions, pray for God to show you any error in your thinking and then just be open to whatever He makes known to you.

Some of us have been wearing beautiful shoes that are killing our feet. For some, the pain has extended to leg and even back pain. We have wardrobes closets full of outer beauty, but each time we put something beautiful on, we're simply masking the pain or struggle which needs to be purged. It's time to take off all of the false pretenses. Dressing up to make yourself feel better is a temporary solution to a long-term issue and it won't last. Dressing down is no better. If you're a star, be a star – dazzle and allow the world to see you in all of God's glory. There have been many people who compliment me because I don't "look like I've had six children". There have also been many who degrade me for the very same reason. I'm not messy enough for them, my clothes don't look "mommy" enough. At one point, I tried to respond to those comments, but only found myself unhappy with a boring wardrobe that didn't come off as genuinely me and made my husband think I was depressed! Be yourself – shine. If you're feeling broken it's okay to pull yourself together and dress up a bit. But don't be deceived – make it a point to deal with what's happening on the inside and know that the wholeness and wellness within, will inevitably dress up the outside. Good shoes are pretty, but good feet are priceless!

CHAPTER 3

ONE OF THESE THINGS IS NOT LIKE THE OTHER

I've always prided myself on being a bit of a chameleon. I moved around a lot over the years and as a result, learned to adapt to a variety of people and environments. I lived in places of concentrated poverty and I lived among wealth and luxury. As a self-guiding principle, I decided at an early age that I didn't want to become just another spec in the sea of various people and environments I'd move through. Instead, I put my energy into being genuine and transparent in who I was. Usually this worked well and I eventually adopted a mantra: "I could wear blue jeans and a t-shirt to a black tie affair and be perfectly at home." I was pleased with my ability to be accepted or rejected on the basis of who I was and either way was alright with me. That is, until I decided to make Christ the head of my life.

"He who will follow me must lay down his own life, in order to gain it." (Matt. 16:25)

With God at the head of my life, I began to notice multiple occasions and environments where I could FEEL my dissimilarity in a way that was just unpleasant. I would ask God, "Are you serious?" I had been following His plan for my life, but after a conversion experience, I became uncomfortably aware that in my authentic skin, I no longer fit in. I would be surrounded with people and customs that were so different from me I wasn't sure I would ever assimilate. Moving to my husband's hometown was one such experience and perhaps the most challenging of its kind, in my life.

The most grueling facets of this particular move were amplified ten times over, the moment I answered the Call to ministry. My Pastor and I agreed that it was time for me to pursue licensing as a Missionary. It required a few years of observation, lots of reading and learning and all the things they never write in the book, but will be experienced. While sitting in class just weeks before the board exam, the instructor posed a question to class. We were reminded that our license (and integrity) depended on the answer. Her question went something like this: "Each of you is here because you believe God has called you to be a missionary. There is no missionary without a mission; so please tell us what mission God has called you to in service for Christ." I drifted into my own thoughts: This instructor had the power to determine my fate in just a few weeks. I expected that truth to make me nervous but surprisingly I remained calm. I knew in my heart that God had called me and while I couldn't see the entire picture, I could finally talk about that Calling with a certain degree of confidence. One by one, the ladies told of their heart-breaking pasts complete with poverty, fatality and other unbelievable atrocities they had survived. I began reflecting on my life. I remembered a joyful childhood of talent shows, weekends in the park and family at every turn. I wondered if I really had what it would take to relate to so many others who had experienced the types of irreparable pain that people in the room had described. Would anyone would even care what I had to say? My life seemed like a breeze compared to their stories! (I was once again, throwing God an "I'm Sorry... You were wrong" moment). And then it struck me "Why should I be sorry for the life God gave me?" Did I have the audacity to tell God that He had made some mistake because I didn't suffer enough? An overwhelming sense of conviction overcame me in the moments that followed.

After waiting patiently as each woman poured out her heart about the beauty that had come from the ashes of her own life, the instructor looked squarely into my eyes as if to indicate there was no one left. There was plenty of time left before the class was over, so I had no chance of getting out of it. "And what has God called you to do?" her voice crooned. I swallowed hard on the lump that had formed in my throat. A mix of frustration and terror gripped my shoulders as if they were pinned to my neck. My eyes welled up with tears and my face turned beet red as I suddenly screeched out, "I don't fry chicken!"

> *My eyes welled up with tears and my face turned beet red as I suddenly screeched out, "I don't fry chicken!"*

Shaken by my own reaction, my next move was no smoother. I looked around the room pausing to observe the eyes of everyone who was staring at me by this time. Before I could get ahold of myself I heard myself repeat this very awkward and seemingly senseless statement. In just a slightly softer voice I wept and uttered, "I don't fry chicken". With what looked like an attempt not to burst into laughter, or perhaps not call in a mental health arrest, the instructor calmly floated towards me and placed her hand on my shoulder and said, "Do you want to tell us more about that?" As soon as I could stop stammering over the knots in my stomach and the endless tears that were sliding steadily down my cheeks I managed to pull myself together enough to explain.

Until just a few years before then I was, I thought, pretty much in charge of my life. I hung out with people that I chose and ate the kinds of foods that I liked. When I could, I spent my time around people with energy that I thrived in and on whom I could depend for motivation. I surrounded myself with people who wanted the same kinds of great things in life that I did and quite often they were hanging out in boat clubs, golf courses and sushi bars. My natural west-coast palette for food was undoubtedly matured and I wasn't much of a chicken-fryer when it came to home-cooked meals. I preferred soup and Paninis, gourmet pizzas, flavorful veggie-dishes and rice pilaf or couscous. One problem, I married a man who loved southern-fried chicken, home-made mashed potatoes and country collards; he could eat this three or four nights per week. I guess I expected the same multi-cultural mix of food and culture to surface at some point – after all we had moved to New York. Not, this New York. This was Upstate - the town of white-hots, salt potatoes and Southern migrants. Many of the people I met could throw down in the pots; it wasn't uncommon to visit his relatives any night of the week and smell oxtail or pork chops and gravy, macaroni and cheese and all the fixens' to go with it. I liked the food, but wasn't a huge fan of eating it every night. I could even make some of it and it didn't taste too bad. Still, I smothered my feelings because I didn't want to offend anyone.

Our children, however, wanted daddy's cooking. Can you blame them? It seemed like everyone around us wanted one kind of food and my palette was completely different. But this wasn't just about food. I struggled to find a circle of friends with the same interests and drive as me. I didn't feel warmly received, but instead closely inspected and cautiously tolerated until this person or that one had made up their mind about me. Feeling so out of place, I implored God for months; "Why do you have me here when I don't fit in and clearly don't have what it takes to fit in?" It was the same distorted spirit that had snuck into my mind concerning the mission God had for me and in the middle of that classroom. Somehow, I had merged the two issues together! Everyone else had some awful experience to share about conquering demons or surviving some type of abuse which led them to their calling – they would be able to turn back and help others who were going through a similar situation. I couldn't pretend that was my calling if I tried. One thing God made me was sincere. As much as I wanted to pretend I was called to walk the streets and pray for the homeless or bring words of comfort to prisoners or prepare meals for those who are unable to provide for themselves, God had made it perfectly clear that He was calling me to another territory altogether. That didn't mean I couldn't be helpful in those services, but it did mean I would have to face my calling in its entirety if I wanted to please God. I began to share with the class how God showed me the tumultuous nature of the lives led by board room executives and politicians. He took me to the homes of presidents and community leaders who have families that miss them for long hours spent in the offices of people who may not truly be invested in the organizational mission. I've sat among the bureaucracies of 'we would fix it, but for the politics' tables where people want to do right but are not willing to risk reputation for the sake of the greater good. God had called me to be a light and an example of His peace, righteousness and integrity in these very places where politics and religion don't intermingle. This wasn't some vision of grandeur wherein I would be applauded or even welcomed because I come with the peace of God. But in fact, I would be rejected, misunderstood and even mistreated for God's sake. Other missionaries would risk their lives in countries where they could be killed for speaking the name of Christ. I would risk my paycheck and reputation in companies where 'spirituality' was the new safe word and the name of God caused discomfort and sensitivity. By comparison, I didn't think my calling or my character was noble enough. I was ashamed to speak out about it. I hadn't heard any sermons in service about praying for the prosperous or visiting with the powerful to tend to their needs. So much emphasis had always been given to the downtrodden or marginalized needs in society. It's pretty easy to sympathize with people who are poor, ill or otherwise disenfranchised. I learned though, that the spiritual and emotional needs of affluent people didn't seem to get the same level of sensitivity.

And while there may not be a multitude of others with a mission like my own, I know I'm not alone. "I don't fry chicken" was a cry for support when it felt like I had played along for far too long; conceding to the styles and behaviors of those around me in order to fit in. I may not have a Mother Theresa calling for the least, the last and the lost, but I learned that I was well able to appreciate the impoverished mindset of a woman who wasn't esteemed at home and so became an Executive tyrant in the office. God used me to encourage a man who was sick with fear and didn't believe he could stand for right in the face of a decision that could have cost him the next election. I have been a friend with people who didn't know or believe in the God that I serve, and pioneering community work came out of the association. I've been an ear to people with fatal diagnoses and spouses who walked out on them. People who once believed, were revived in their faith and others found an appetite to know more about God. All of this was happening on golf courses and in executive offices and vacation homes! Often times I was ministering to people who had means I could only dream about, and it seemed strange that God would give me such an unusual mission. Even so, I found out that He also gave me everything I needed to bring light, encouragement and truth to those who need Him. (Rom 8:30) I've always believed, but He showed me that love does not discriminate. While I hadn't known many others who were called like me before then, I've learned of so many since and I realized that the Call wasn't so strange after all. In fact, our instructor later opened up and bonded with me over an identical call upon her life. I was just amazed!

The conditions of human need may be different but the essence of the needs remain fairly the same.

It didn't happen quickly, but over years and various experiences God led me to an understanding that was so profound and yet so simple: The conditions of human need may be different but the essence of the needs remain fairly the same. Pain, sadness, hunger, fear all have the same nature no matter what the circumstances. People in private planes need God just like people in homeless shelters. I couldn't see that before. I thought the more noble causes had a real kind of pain, while the causes that were compelling my heart were somehow less important. I was looking at things the wrong way. Sometimes, God wants us to make a small adjustment in our vision, like tilting your head just a bit in order to see it differently. Other times we need to make a full about face. I was in need of an about face. When I stopped comparing myself to others, I started asking God how to move and what to do. Then suddenly things were in focus – spiritual focus that is. I was being commissioned to be a light in the working world in corporate offices and private boardrooms. I was being called to show God's love in the workforce, in my home and neighborhood and anywhere else where the comforts of this world might give way to complacency or apathy towards humankind. I was too busy seeking examples of how to become this Missionary. Until then, I thought Missionaries (who mattered anyway) helped downtrodden people. Then God affirmed that yes, that is what they do – only my perception of who that was, was too narrow. God showed me the ailments that plague rich people and well-offs just as much as those who are less fortunate in terms of material things. And I became glad for His calling. I no longer felt like I wasn't qualified to do His bidding. I was reminded that my Calling comes from the One who made me. And that was enough for me.

I realize that not every place I go will welcome me. I am fully aware that everyone who shakes my hand doesn't wish well for my future. I know that not everyone who comes to our home, is happy for our blessings and I also know that not everyone who calls out Lord Lord, believes on the name of Jesus. God showed me that I can be in this knowledge and love and live freely anyhow. Being among people and environments where you don't neatly fit in may cause you to stand out - but you don't have to stand down.

All things work together for good to them that love The Lord and are called according to His good purpose. (Romans 8:28) Your purpose is not the final culmination of some destiny you will reach one day. It is found within each moment and each interaction of your day – every day. The traits that make you different are the very ones required for you to be able to respond to the needs of others in your life. Don't succumb to those doubtful thoughts about why you're in the place you are. Seek the Lord for clarity. Ask for wisdom and patience to understand how you can be a light there. Then trust God and watch it manifest!

Momentary misgivings, reservations and doubt can be reduced to nothing if we shift our thoughts towards God and His promise to accomplish all that He has set into motion. If you can move past this moment, you can move past this mountain.

- Can you "fry chicken"? Will you choose to stand out or stand alone in the unique gifts and abilities that God has given you?
- What attributes about yourself have you dismissed because you don't believe they are noble enough to make a difference for Christ?

Maybe your past doesn't include a history of abuse or neglect. Perhaps you have never been addicted to drugs or criminal behaviors. Maybe you've never seen the inside of a prison. Perhaps you never will. Thank God for His grace, then acknowledge the experiences that you have had as being counted worthy of God's calling on your life. (Eph. 4:1)

CHAPTER 4

IT'S LONELY AT THE TOP

Alone. Solitude. Seclusion. These are states of being that are often accompanied by serenity. When someone chooses to be alone, it's usually attributed to his or her desire to be away from the bustle and commotion of life. Have you ever desired to be alone? The word even sounds somewhat inviting – alone. Maybe you are reading this book right now, alone. Go ahead. Say the word… *aalllloooonnne*. Nice, huh? Now try 'lonely'. It doesn't quite roll off of your tongue with the same warmth as "alone". Aloneness is the state of being apart from or without company. Loneliness is a feeling that arises when you believe that you are separated from others, but don't desire to be. The two words are related but what one yields is diabolically opposed to the other. You can be alone and not be lonely. You can also be lonely in a crowd. Jesus must've felt this way much of His time here on earth.

When God calls you to do something, He calls you alone. You may be surrounded by a loving family. You can be married and blissfully smitten with your spouse. Still, God's calling on you… is on you alone. That can sometimes cause you to *feel* lonely. God's ways take on a higher standard of excellence than the world. Are you a bit of a perfectionist? Are you the person who wants to practice just one more time? Is "do it right or don't do it at all" your motto? If so, you are likely driven to excellence. When you have to work with others who don't perform with similar standards, it can be frustrating – causing you to once again feel alone. *Why doesn't anyone else care (like I do)?* Before you dismiss everyone else as "not getting it" take a moment to realize that something may be happening inside of you. There is a separation taking place but it's not physical. Maybe your faith is growing exponentially. Maybe your appetite for holiness is increasing. Could be any of a number of events that will grow you at a pace beyond the people around you. Changes like this can isolate you from others who just aren't in the same place. Still, you can embrace that aloneness by celebrating God's spirit within you. It's okay to want perfection. In fact we should be striving for it! So long as we desire perfection for the sake of glorifying God and not ourselves, we are on the right track. It is helpful though, to recognize that not everyone is striving for that same goal at the exact same time as you. Can you be gracious with others and disciplined with yourself in this season? Will you accept that there are people who want to succeed, but may not have the faith to move forward? Resist the temptation to shake their marbles loose and turn your thoughts towards what's going on inside of you.

It's heart-wrenching to be in the knowledge of God's goodness, yet watch people around you seem to idle in neutral as if He wasn't the best thing since sliced bread. As God's attributes come alive in you, it's important to realize that the same may not yet be stirred up in others. This can place you in a class all by yourself, but you don't have to feel lonely. God is with you. A host of angels are with you. And your separation is happening for your own good.

> *A higher standard of excellence may separate you from other people. What changes are happening inside of you that may set you apart from your peers or loved ones?*

One Sunday morning as I rose with a dozen teenagers to line up across the ornate wooden altar for the morning review of our Sunday

School text, I gazed out across several rows of adult students who seemed ready to hear our usual 3-minute call and response. That particular day however, the students were ready for anything but the usual. They asked questions and they were really engaged in the lesson so they were ready with memory verses and demonstrations that would wow the adult classes, or so they hoped. They were ready and it showed as they stood eagerly and spoke clearly into the microphone throughout the entire three minutes. We finished our public review and it was time for the weekly Sunday School march – a time when everyone could participate in marching down the aisle to drop their pennies in the collection bucket while singing a happy Sunday School Song. I prompted the entire congregation to stand and join the two youth who had volunteered to lead the march. As the young ladies readily leaned into the microphones and started singing, I stood behind them and joined in quietly enough that their voices would be heard over my own. "*Sunday Schoool Sunday Schoool Sunday Schoool Sunday Schoooool... Sunday School is marching ooonnnn. S-U-N-D-A-Y-S-C-H-O-O-L Sunday School is marching ooonnnnn*". As we began the second verse, I looked out into the congregation where the adult class was gathered – some standing others resting in the seats and chatting amongst themselves. Maybe three of them were singing. I leaned into the mic and as kindly as I could manage, 'invited' them to join us in singing or clapping along. With each round I thought about the melody's words and our morning lesson. I Corinthians Chapter 12. 'We are all members in one body' and all the parts are needed for a healthy and whole community. My heart dropped. I couldn't figure out why the adults weren't as enthusiastic about closing the lesson, as the children and I. Didn't they have the same text that morning? And then it hit me. Though we were all gathered together for learning and worship, not everyone was there with a zeal to do so. That shouldn't take away from the joy and fervor inside of me.

Separation is a part of life. From the time we are born, people places and things will come and go with the purposes to which they are assigned. Consider Jonah who was alone in the desert after running far away from the place God commissioned him to visit, Nineveh. (Jon. 1:3) God made sure Jonah knew He was with him throughout his runaway attempt.

Or Paul who helped to establish and support so many of the New Testament churches, yet was ostracized by the members who felt like he had gotten too big for his britches. How alone must he have felt when in prison cells he continued to write letters to those same churches encouraging them to continue their trust and works in the Lord. (Gal. 4:12-20)

What about Esther who, with no idea of what lie ahead, left her family to live in the King's court until the day she was selected to become Queen? Even with all the special treatment granted her, it must've been frightening to move into a palace among strangers only to be selected as their leader and later to be told you would have to risk your life so that others would not die. (Esth. 8)

The bible is full of examples of people who were chosen by God to do great things – alone. This hasn't been, and isn't today, always about being the best or caring too much. This separation can also look like:

- The one black male in a graduating class, employment division or affluent field of study
- The student who the teacher *always* calls on when no one else will raise a hand
- The person for whom promotions come quickly, or in succession, but with little visible evidence for why and how
- The vibrant and happily married couple
- The first young man or woman in the family to graduate high school, and college.
- A bi-racial child who isn't black enough for her black peers or white enough for her white peers

Getting the picture?

There are just some people whose lives are predestined to stand out in some form or another. In my early career, I worked in executive suites while crossing paths with my family or friends only in cafeterias and hallways. Yes, we worked at the same company, but rarely did many other people who looked like me, work on the same floor. I would see someone I knew when the mail cart was passing through and I'd think to myself, why don't more people I know work on the executive level floors? I would sit with others who looked like me for 30 minutes in the cafeteria over lunch but as soon as that cattle whistle blew, they'd go their way and I'd go my way. Maybe I overthought this. Perhaps there was no significant reason I was the only black person or the only female or the only person under the age of 40 in my 'suite'. Still, I often wondered, "When will I see more of my peers at this level of the company?"

If this sounds like something you've experienced, you may belong to an exclusive club for which you did not sign up. Sure you put in the effort – the schooling, the networking, the stand-out interview - but you didn't really sign up for such exclusivity. As the discomfort of your new membership begins to settle in, you must be prepared to walk through doors that no one else can enter but you. There will be news and experiences that you share enthusiastically, but no one will seem as excited about them as you. There will be standards you uphold, and no one else will maintain those standards with the same level of integrity, as you. You will see yourself as more and more distinguished from even the most common groups with whom you've been connected. Yes, even family and close friends will seem like a herd going in one direction, when you are compelled to go another way. If the crowd

it may be time to accept that you have been not only called, but you have been chosen.

starts to thin out as you progress from one experience to another, it may be time to accept that you have been not only called, but you have been chosen.

When God chooses you - calls you apart for His glory - He chooses your mind, body and spirit. That means the people around you may or may not understand what is going on. They may love what they see God doing in your life and wish to be a part in some way. However, just like luggage limits on airplanes that need to carry the right amount *and type* of weight, there are limits to the amount *and type* of weight you can take to the next level of your life.

There will be issues that you can't vet with just anyone; sometimes not even the person in your own bed. There will be celebrations you'll want to share, but no human suitable with whom to rejoice. It's not that everyone is against you; it could be that everyone isn't meant to take on what you take on. In these moments, turn to God and ask Him to show you if there is someone with whom you can talk. Quite often that someone will be Him.

Having a higher calling on your life means you will remain in the world but you will not be in harmony with the world's ways. (John 17:15-17) This requires a balance that can only be achieved with God at the head of each priority in your life. If you're going to follow God's plan for your life, you must be willing to give up the comforts of connecting with people. I didn't say give up the connections; just the comforts associated with them – talking out your problems to someone, hearing reassuring words that let you know you're on the right track, having someone with whom you can bounce ideas around… you know – comforts. People you used to hang out with will miss the "old you" and feel like you've abandoned them in your new way of life. As you discover how to be the true you that God created, you'll start to seem peculiar to people around you. Well, Jesus stuck out like a sore thumb among the people of his time - why not you?

Now back to those church folk who turned on me, uh… I mean Paul. He had a passion for what he did and he executed his calling with intense dedication. Jesus had some disciples and others who traveled with him throughout his ministry. Paul's posse could be counted on one hand, with a few fingers leftover. After a while, there weren't many people who rolled out the red carpet for Paul when they heard he was coming. In fact, he began to ask and inquire for room at people's houses (the unbelievers) in his latter missions and then eventually he was imprisoned, but he continued to write letters and encourage others in God's word. Even there he remained encouraged and passionate about Christ and he won souls to Heaven in his fervor for God.

The very same people who cheered you on at the beginning of your journey, may well be the same obstacles that come up against you as God promotes you in the Kingdom and in the world. We have the kind of God who will spread out a bountiful table for you, right in front of your enemies. He will even take your enemies and cause them to be your footstool as you go higher and higher in your journey! That's not the kind of stuff that's likely to win you a huge fan-following.

When, as a result of your elevation, others begin to fall off and leave you standing alone, remember three truths that will set your emotions straight.

1. **You may feel lonely, but you are not alone.** God gave us certain feelings so that we could relate to Jesus and admit that we need relationship and dependency on Him. When you feel lonely, think of God. Think about the angels he has assigned to minister to you and protect you. (Ps 91:11-12) Embrace the time alone as a chance to learn more about yourself through God's eyes. Become real friends with God and you'll never be alone.

2. **Discretion is invaluable for leadership.** When God has you in a place of solitude for a long time, you may eventually want to confide in someone. Proverbs wisdom however, reveals the dangers of not tempering your enthusiasm because there are sometimes ill-intentioned people in the midst. It's sad but true. Still, not everyone is out for your destruction. The enemy certainly is and he will use any

available source to do so. Allow the Holy Spirit to guide you to safe places for sharing your plans, or to help you keep your lips closed when it's not time to share – you won't explode, promise!

3. **Keep your eyes on the prize.** When the air gets harder to breathe and the company begins to thin out, don't look down. Look up towards the Heavens instead and remind yourself of where you're going. Sure it can seem lonely up there but the view is incredible if you can keep climbing. You may not see the same faces you once did or even the same places, but God never takes you from bad to worse without an expected end. In His hands we go from glory to glory!

"One can never consent to creep when one feels an impulse to soar."
Helen Keller 07/08/1896

CHAPTER 5

THE PENALTY (AND PAIN) OF PRIVILEGE

God help you if you are an ugly girl
Course too pretty is also your doom
Cause everyone harbors a secret hatred
For the prettiest girl in the room
*And God help you if you are a **phoenix*** * italics added*
And you dare to rise up from the ash
A thousand eyes will smolder with jealousy
While you are just flying back

32 Flavors Written by Ani DiFranco (1995): Later covered by Alana Davis (1998)

From biblical writings to common satire and stereotypes, Americans have commonly assigned the notion of conceit or insensitivity to affluent people. Not everyone attains wealth for the sake of having it all to themselves. There are philanthropists who use their resources to improve conditions for others who are less fortunate. The Red Crosses, United Ways and local food pantries of this world wouldn't exist without them. Still it's easy to condemn or shame the well-to-do because you don't associate golf courses and yacht clubs with any sort of struggle or brokenness. The bible has a lot to say about the love of money and the destruction that derives from it. But notice, God doesn't extend a message about evil money, but rather an evil heart. (I Tim 6:10) A man's heart is what determines the distribution of his wealth and whether it will glorify him or God. Sure, it will be easier for a camel to get through the eye of a needle than for a rich man to enter the kingdom of heaven. (Mark 10:25) But the context of these verses have more to do with how easily a rich person can start to put his faith in his wealth and its benefits, instead of relying on God who makes the wealth possible. It's that slippery slope concept. This happens to people around the world. Still, the text isn't meant to imply that all or even most wealthy people are greedy, self-centered elitists who don't know or care about the problems facing the world. They have the same problems; just with different circumstances and often higher amounts of risk.

It must be nice to be rich. Smart people are so arrogant. Pretty people get by on their good looks. Stereotypes like this have had a tendency to glide flippantly through the ages of time. It's difficult though, to find someone who will challenge the mean spirit behind them. Sure a good person would defend a young girl who is being teased about her homely shoes, but are we just as likely to stick up for a brainy student who is teased for doing his homework all semester? It's a privilege to be intelligent. Unfortunately not everyone honors privilege. In fact, people who are seen as privileged often face contempt simply because of their advantage – perceived or real. Why shouldn't the student receive the same concern as the young girl?

Privilege-

(n.): a right or benefit that is given to some people and not to others; (n.): a special opportunity to do something that makes you proud; (n.): the advantage that wealthy and powerful people have over other people in a society. OR (n.): a right or immunity granted as a peculiar benefit, advantage, or favor: prerogative (Webster Online Dictionary 08/28/15)

What do you know? A privilege sounds a lot like a blessing. Prosperity, intellect, good looks – these are all attributes that God can bestow on anyone. Even so, He doesn't give them to everyone. Possessing them can certainly provide some advantages which might seem unfair and even result in resentment. That said, it's hurtful to be treated with resentment simply because you are privileged in some way. It's upsetting when you are regarded as if you don't have substance because you're beautiful looking. The anguish felt when a single parent immediately dismisses your counsel because you're happily married and you "couldn't possibly understand what she's going through" can be unbearable. This kind of wrongful speculation can, subtly and over time, cause you to feel like you don't deserve the blessings you've been granted. You may begin to feel as if you aren't relevant or that your problems seem trivial when compared to others with less advantage than you.

Have you ever been challenged or made to feel like a snob because you embrace progress or desire success? That seems like twisted thinking when you consider the life God intends for those who follow His plan for their lives. "Stay on the path that the Lord your God has commanded you to follow. Then you will live long and prosperous lives in the land you are about to enter and occupy." (Deut. 5:33)

there is no reason to apologize for the favor, blessings and even privileges that befall you in this life.

With righteous motives, there is no reason to apologize for the favor, blessings and even privileges that befall you in this life.

God is the architect of our lives which means He gets to decide who gets what, and when. When you consider this fact, two very important considerations should come to mind:

1. When someone other than you is blessed:

God's Word lets us know that He reigns on the just and the unjust. (Matt 5:45) It becomes a little harder then, to resent favor in someone else's life simply because you don't believe they deserve it. Plus, you never know which side of that equation you may be on one day! Still, it can be difficult if you witness someone who doesn't seem to care whether God knows them or not and they look like they're prospering. Meanwhile you can barely catch a break and you're doing all you can to be pleasing in His sight. This is a perfect opportunity for the devil to manipulate that little green speck in your eye and make it seem as though you're missing out on something. It's also a perfect opportunity for God to perfect the spiritual fruit that will later be required in your journey – it's just not your turn today. Can you be good to someone who doesn't seem to deserve it? How about when you believe you are deserving, and it feels like no one's being good to you? If you're on your way out of your current state, how do you know you won't need that skill – being good to others when no one seems to be good to you? It can feel lonely at the top right? If others seem to be getting all the favor and privilege and you find yourself desiring a piece of it, become future-focused on your own life rather than feature-focused with their current life. Begin to pray and seek God for where He is taking you. Ask for wisdom and understanding in the character traits He is developing during your "off" season. Ask if you are truly in your "off" season or if you just couldn't truly appreciate your own blessings because you were so focused on someone else's. What is God doing in you right now, for the journey and plan He has for your life? Turn your flashlight away from others and look to yourself, your inner self, to see if God is doing something in you.

It's not easy to see things the way God does. His ways are so much higher than yours; His thoughts too! (Isa 55:8-9) But that's why it's so important to turn to Him with gratefulness for things you may tend to reduce in importance. They may be the very things He wants to use to manifest your blessing.

> *What if our blessings come through raindrops? What if our healing comes through tears? What if a thousand sleepless nights are what it takes to know You're near? What if trials of this life, are your mercies in disguise?*

Performed by Laura Story 2011. Writer(s): Laura Mixon Story, Liz Story

Copyright: Story Duke Music, Laura Stories, New Spring Publishing Inc., Warner-tamerlane Publishing Corp)

2. When you're the one being blessed

Blessings are from God. If you believe this than you may agree that it's only logical to consult Him with how to manage and enjoy it. First say thank you God; then ask Him, "Now what would you like for me to do with this?" A well-off business man decided he wanted to purchase a helicopter and install a private landing pad in his backyard. The neighborhood was in an uproar. Complaints followed about the potential for noise, pollution and other aggravations this might cause. By all means, this man should be able to build whatever he likes on his own property and enjoy it too. But would God see this as the means for doing so? God sees the long hours, frequent travel required to maintain the businesses and the limited time with family, so it may be His desire for the businessman to have the leisure and convenience of such a purchase. God though, may offer a more considerate location from which it would fly and land.

God is love and love is not self-seeking. See, it's not the actions of this man that would dishonor God but the intent of his heart to carry out the actions. This is why Timothy's letters to the church emphasized that it is not money itself that is evil, but the love of it – because desiring anything more than God is idolatry. (I Tim 6:10) This directly conflicts with the freedom that a life in Christ offers because it neglects the responsibility that comes with that freedom. More about that in the next chapter.

Every rich person wasn't born with a silver spoon in his or her mouth. Have you ever considered the discretion of many people who live under the radar of the public eye? Often they perform charitable acts in secret; in fact that's just how the Bible suggests we do. This means, we shouldn't assume that rich people aren't thoughtful and generous concerning the needs of those less fortunate, just because they're rich. We've got to stop assigning – even in our thoughtlife – stereotypes to people on the basis of what we see. God *wants* prosperous, successful epistles throughout the earth so people can know His love and His power. (See Prov 22:29) He will establish people with assets and resources who manage their wealth so that the needs of those less fortunate can be met. It's philanthropy at its best. Unfortunately, rather than celebrate privilege, our society seems to magnify the pride or abuse of some advantaged people and many have come to regard that, as the standard for all. There should be no penalty for simply being blessed. It becomes the responsibility of the blessed individual to use his or her advantages for good. Whether they accept that responsibility is between them and their god.

God places a light inside each of us. Discovering that light and its power, can only happen when we take our eyes off of the gift, and begin to focus on the One who gave the gifts to us – the Creator. It does no good to try and modify what God made as if He didn't get it right the first time. People will tell you to be yourself all the time; still everyone won't respond positively when you do. Don't think of it as if some strange thing has happened only to you. (1 Pet. 4:12) Jesus experienced the very same persecution during his time here on earth. God doesn't make mistakes. His light inside of us cannot be consumed by darkness. (John 1:5) In our human nature, we are that darkness. But with the nature of Christ living on the inside of us, there's no good reason to conceal the privileges that his blessings sanction in our lives. If your light isn't causing some discomfort in this world then it isn't the true light of God at work; it could be you. Glorify God with your gifts and use your advantage for good even if there are some discomforts along the way; your life and the world around you will be better for it.

Some time ago, one of my daughters came to me surprised at what her peers were saying; that she "lives in the suburbs so what does she know?" Their words assumed that she had no skin in the game when it came to 'keeping it real', because she didn't live where they lived. She was hurt and offended. Eventually she started questioning herself as she became unsure about whether she could genuinely relate to those or other children who came from different places than her. I observed this pattern of assumption and speculation as I witnessed it play out for people who were more fortunate than those around them.

A CFO drives to work in his little red corvette. He speaks of his privately-schooled children with hope and admiration. He shares the newest family dilemma over a holiday trip to The Hamptons or New York City and the issue of today is which doggie daycare will make the wife happy. You get the picture. It's hard to empathize with someone in this situation if the issues flowing through your own head sound more like: Should I buy food for the house or pick up my insulin prescription? Can't do both. In this comparison, your heart strings may feel a tougher pull for the person who has to choose between food and medicine, than for the one who is choosing a daycare for his dog while he whisks his family off for the holidays. And the rich man doesn't get the hug that day.

It's important not to regard people only in light of their current circumstances. Humans are not that simple. You are not the sum of your economic state. You are not wholly characterized by your talents or your callings. Your past contributed to your present, but does not alone, define it. There are visible and invisible attributes that make you who you are. If you agree with this for your own life, than the same truth holds for the lives of people around you, whether affluent or in poverty. That CFO planning his holiday trip, may be doing so because it's the last year he'll be able to travel due to a worsening health condition. Or maybe he puts so much into his leisure experience with the family because their time together is rare and precious. There aren't too many Chief Financial Officers that clock in at 9 and clock out at 5. Perhaps he wasn't always rich, but built his wealth over time and started out making hand-to-mouth decisions; could his sharing this holiday dilemma with you be an opportunity to increase your faith and hope for a brighter future. If it could happen for him, why not you? Rather than dismiss his dilemma as not being redeeming enough, take time to consider what else there is to the man, that you may not know and begin to seek for similarities. The enemy seems to love putting hostility, no matter how small, between people who have the opportunity to better one another. In this case, you might develop an oversimplified opinion of someone based on just what you see in front of you. It's up to you to see past this smoke and mirrors act, to the truth. Everyone has a set of circumstances that brought them to their present state. Would you agree?

- Are you considerate of other people's misfortune because you can see it?
- Are you less sympathetic with beautiful people, wealthy people or otherwise affluent individuals because you can't easily see their hardship?

Marginalization is the same whether you are privileged or not. Could this be the new face of charity?

It never feels good to be relegated because of someone's incomplete view of you. People, privileged and unprivileged alike, are multidimensional and should not be regarded through one single feature of their existence. God blesses whoever He wants. When you take issue with a person's favor, you're not raising an issue with man, you're raising an issue with God. (Rom. 9:14-16)

CHAPTER 6

BEING FREE, NOT DEFIANT

Don't you love it when some really obscure truth about life becomes made known to you resulting in some type of new freedom? You don't even have to be saved to relate to this, though it only amplifies if you are. Epiphanies are all around us, often hovering patiently in the face of each repeated mistake we are about to make. They are like mystic oracles waiting for us to reach out and grab ahold, wearing small tags that read, "Pull Me" or "Grab ahold". When we finally do grab and pull, we unleash their power to emancipate us from the patterns that have kept us in dark or painful experiences. For example if you don't like to argue, coming to the realization that one person can't hold a debate, will free you from fighting back with words and consequently peace comes more quickly. Or maybe you believed for years that you were bound to repeat some of the same mistakes your parents and their parents before them did; only to one day discover that if you change your behaviors you will change the possible outcomes. Or when you come to the understanding that God's plan for your life is much better than yours and you finally release the controls; then you begin to have all the things your heart desired –even though you didn't know you wanted them. These epiphanies tend to bring about a healing in your thoughts and emotions. But did you know they can also bring with them, a sense of frustration. Why didn't I gain this understanding sooner? Why wasn't I set free before all that suffering?!

In this way, the Bible becomes a manual providing oodles of methods for dealing with every day issues. Specifically, Proverbs contains oodles of wisdom about life stuff and how to deal with it. What's life stuff? It's the stuff that life throws at you and the questions that your mind develops when you become discouraged or frustrated by it. You don't control when it comes or even how. Learning how to correctly perceive life stuff can lead to correctly managing it. Revelation knowledge is given to you as a gift from God to help you navigate life stuff. Even so, its timetable isn't always its most desirable feature. Remember watching The Wizard of Oz and the look on Dorothy's face when the good witch Glenda told her she had the power to go home all along; that all she had to do was believe and click her heels? Dorothy was shocked and elated! She only needed to figure out how to say goodbye to all the new friends she'd made in her tumultuous journey. Even that was a good problem to have. I, on the other hand, had re-written that particular scene playing it out a little more realistically with me starring as Dorothy. *Good Witch:* "Why Dorothy dear… you've had the power to go home anytime you liked." (big smile and glance and the shimmery red shoes) *Dorothy, or… me*: "What?! I got these shoes the moment I landed here! And you've known this the whole time? So you've been watching me suffer all this time and you're just now deciding to share this little jewel with me? What kind of good witch are you? I'm outta here!"

In my less-wise version of this classic family film, I had written off the very person who gave me what I wanted most. In fact, I had written off the whole town of Oz – lollipop kids and all! Why wasn't it enough to have received the answer when it came? I would still get what mattered the most… to go home. Whatever, I was out for blood. Somebody knew how to avoid all that pain for me but they didn't tell me. I felt mocked, made a fool and, well I felt as if I was part of someone's evil lab experiment to see if I could survive. It was time for payback and I was out for blood! Only problem was, I had vengeful eyes for the wrong people. If anyone deserved my anger, it was the enemy not my allies. I just didn't realize they weren't one in the same.

Any time you reach another milestone to become a greater and better you, the devil gets upset. He doesn't want to see us at our best. We are at our best when can confidently operate in our gifts and blessings. If the enemy can find one point of vulnerability, he will use his same old smoke n' mirrors act to try and hinder us from shining. Like the serpent in Eve's ear when he tried to convince her that God had withheld some wonderful knowledge that she should have also been granted. (Gen 3:4) Anger, even a little anger, is an excellent point of vulnerability for the enemy to do his work. He can work with anger by tricking us into doubting ourselves or others. Why didn't the good witch tell Dorothy sooner that she could have gone home? The truth is, Dorothy's character was flawed and with each new encounter she was given a chance to grow and develop. *My* Dorothy may have undone all that progress because she would have abused her newfound liberty by lashing out at her allies.

God, His Word and His plan for us are our allies. When he sets new understanding in our hearts, it isn't so that we might get angry and forget to honor his laws. Jesus himself explained that he didn't come to abolish the law, but to fulfill it. (Matt. 5:17-19) Instead, we should be grateful for the new freedom and be wise and prudent stewards with it. The only entitlements in the liberty of Christ are for things that are pure, holy and righteous. God's freedoms don't grant us the right to become empowered, self-ruling titans whose light no longer shines for Him. Truth condemns a lie all by itself. Our man-made forms of vengeance are never required to repay the damage committed by a lie.

Was Dorothy too selfish to see that she wasn't the only beneficiary of her journey? Didn't the Lion, the Tin man and the Scarecrow also discover their greatness in the end? Come to think of it, though she had to fight for it, didn't Dorothy eliminate Oz' greatest enemy and liberate the entire community from the fear and injustice under which they had been living? When you think of it that way, it seems a little silly to be upset at not clicking her heels sooner.

Jesus sets up the liberating truth through his teaching in Matthew 15:5-6. Today it might look like this: You are extremely faithful about paying your tithes. Out of obedience to God's laws, you are committed to not missing this one each payday. This week though, you notice that your mother's cabinets are a little empty; still you don't have extra money and you don't even consider taking from your tithes because that's not an honorable exception. Sorry mom, God expects my tithes so you'll just have to tighten your belt this week since I can't buy food for you.

Later, Paul revisits this concept in the way he believed Jesus intended. That same story would continue this way today. One day God shows your heart how it would be more honorable to provide groceries for mom in that situation. You do so and it feels great – plus mom prepares your favorite meal and has you over that week. Do you then begin to release yourself from the duty of paying tithes because you can come up with lots of honorable exceptions? If so, you have become abusive with your new liberty and with the One who gave it to you. (Gal. 5:13 and I Cor. 10:23) Perhaps the pages of this book have revealed some redeeming quality in your own life. Maybe you learned of some legalistic behavior in your life that may have overshadowed the love principle God really desired for you to live out. If so – to God be the glory, the blinders are off!

God wants to give us truths that will allow us to live an enlightened life. This kind of life has been liberated from the traps of the enemy, from the full penalty of sin and from the condemnation or guilt associated with unrighteous behaviors. He [God] wants us to be free, not foolish. This enlightened

> *He [God] wants us to be free, not foolish.*

life does not excuse us from order or rule. In fact it's an even more disciplined lifestyle than the former one with those old self-seeking desires and goals.

Getting new understanding and revelation wisdom from God is like getting your driver's license for the first time. Oh the places you can now go! God's insight gives access to more wonderful experiences and opportunities to shine in this lifetime. You find peace more quickly. Dark days return to joy more readily. You learn how to be gentle in the face of adversity. Love in impossible circumstances becomes once more possible. Still, to whom much is given much more is required (Luke 12:48). So you received the newfound wisdom that simply going to church every time the doors open may not be the key for getting into Heaven; this does not give you a pass to rarely or never go to church. God speaks to each one of our hearts as He grants wisdom and understanding about these and other matters of the heart. It's important to receive the wisdom about life stuff, but it's equally important to understand how to use that new wisdom in order to glorify, and not shame, God.

When scales are removed from our eyes, it's tempting to wonder why they weren't removed sooner. Much like my revised version of The Wizard of Oz, we regard God with thanks and attitude altogether when He redeems us from some erroneous way of thinking; not understanding why He allowed us to go through the agonizing experience for far longer than we would have liked. A better way is to embrace your emancipation in Christ by recognizing the One who made it possible – then your star will be incapable of being concealed by others, even you won't be able to keep it from shining.

In learning I didn't have to keep being sorry about my gifts or about the talents God had given me, I found a new confidence. It came suddenly and yielded a struggle between my flesh and my Spirit not to allow the confidence to be misplaced. I had to remember that my assurance should be placed in Christ and not myself. That would keep me from becoming too indignant about the new freedom God had just made available to me. Even the most astute of disciples, as unbelievable as it seems, can fall for this trick of the enemy. Yep – if it were at all possible the enemy would fool even the elect of God's. (Matt 24:24) In all your getting, get an understanding and allow God to balance out the truth that He has given you.

- Have you ever felt like some great oracle of wisdom was held from you, but dangled over your situation for far too long?
- Have you learned something that caused you to decide you won't do something anymore because God says you don't have to in order to be saved, in order for God to love you, etc.?
- Is this something that God may still desire for you, so that your life or someone else's might be enriched?

CHAPTER 7

MY FINAL APOLOGY

We were born human. The nature of flesh is sinful. With Christ in our lives, we are being perfected daily. Still, until that great reunion-in-the-sky happens, we are a construction site in process. We will look flawed and imperfect. We will stumble from time to time and not execute God's standards the way He demonstrated them through His son Jesus. And for these reasons, there will be PLENTY of events we create that will warrant a sincere apology, to God and to man.

The key is to learn as much about sorrow and repentance as we can, in order to recognize those things for which we should ask forgiveness. Psalm 34:18 says "The Lord is close to the brokenhearted; he rescues those whose spirits are crushed". When we feel like we have breached relationships, with God or man, it's common to feel crushed. That doesn't mean we should manufacture brokenness in our own lives in order to have good standing with God. Destitution doesn't make you any closer to Him. Rather, use gratefulness as a tool to overpower any doubt, confusion or chaos that may arise when you begin to think in those terms.

With this understanding firmly in place, I wrote my final apology to God concerning the issues expressed at the heart of this book:

Good morning God. Thank you for knowing the issues of my heart and for freeing me from the limitations of my own thinking. I can't tell you how great it feels to know I don't have to be ashamed of the many ways you cause me to excel. In fourth grade, it was You who placed me in the gifted and talented classes. You knew what that would mean for my life down the road and I thank you. Before I was born, it was You who decided what my hair, complexion and body-type were going to be... and you took Your sweet time detailing me, thank you. I don't know when, but I'm betting I wasn't even thinking about him when you cradled my husband in your hands and crafted the love, care and wisdom that he has today to be the devout father and husband that he is – we're so lucky. I mean blessed! When I got the job, the one I wasn't even qualified to apply for but you led me through those doors anyway, I just knew it was you who whispered in that Director's ear and placed him in my path. What a wonderful ride that was! And the next job when you used my former enemies as a footstool to position me at a greater advantage – I couldn't have designed that plan myself if I tried. Oh and God I enjoy wearing beautiful clothes and driving a really nice car... having plenty of space in the yard for the kids to play and I really enjoy the many comforts that You provide from time to time so we don't get stuck in a rut. Not everyone realized that they came from You... but I did.

And God – thank you for giving me great communication skills, a heart for hospitality and a love for all kinds of people. I wasn't always so proud of these things at one time. I liked it sort of, but when other people didn't like it, I wished you hadn't made me that way. Do you remember when I made Captain for the Varsity Cheerleading squad in high school, but my best friend made JV, how weird it felt knowing we wouldn't be practicing or performing together? I was ready to quit the squad! I'm so glad she didn't feel the same way. I'm sorry I couldn't see your hand at work there. Oh, and how many times did you make a way for me to step out on faith and lead some noble adventure only to see me refuse and step aside? I stopped loving those adventures because people would say things that hurt. I know you heard them. I'm sorry for letting that stop me from saying yes to you the other times. God thank you for redeeming me always. I'm so glad that I can't be separated from Your love. I'm ready to take a leap Father. I'm ready to face my fears and nose dive into whatever deep waters you have placed before me. Please help me to be wise in doing so. If You're going to blow my mind along the way, help me to be self-controlled enough to receive what You're giving me. God, help me also to never become dull or insensitive to the small wonders you give out from day to day. I really want Your light to shine through me so that other people will come to know You in all of your awesome wonder. So yeah God – I just wanna say I'm sorry it's taken me so long to get to this place, but I'm not sorry that I'm here. I'm grateful and I cannot thank You enough for giving me new eyes to see Your light in a way I never did before. (deep breath) With your help, this is the last time I'll ever regret being the way I am. You made me and I am so honored that you did. Let's illuminate this world, shall we? And of course, You knew I'd say all of that, didn't You?

CHAPTER 8

7 TRUTHS THAT STINK

1. **It's not you, it's God.** There's no such thing as a self-made millionaire. God is the divine conductor of all things. Even when we don't see it, He is working behind the scenes to make sure that certain people come, and go, from our lives. He is orchestrating the times and the conditions by which new opportunities come our way. Coincidence is the term assigned when man cannot explain how a set of conditions comes together in such a way that the man or woman could not have designed more ideally. No coincidence people… that's God. Your identity is no coincidence. The circumstances and conditions that came together to make you who you are today, were no coincidence. The mark of God's workmanship is all over you. While many people take pride in their culture, hometown or some other identifying characteristic, it is identity with Christ that gives you the true mark of distinction. The 100th Psalm reminds us that we didn't make ourselves, but God made us and because there is no error in Him, we can know with certainty that any privileges that may come along as part of our making,

are not by happenstance. They are not the result of our tireless efforts to be all we can be. Acts 17:28 indicates God as the source of all life. "For in him we live and move and exist," If you want to righteously claim the advantages that go along with living a blessed life, you must accept this vital truth. If not, it would be futile to try and accept the truths that follow. Feel free to put the book down and just reflect on the statements in this section alone. Repeat them in your daily affirmations and allow the Holy Spirit to saturate and validate your understanding as you credit God with every ounce of your being.

2. **It's not you, it's them.** Haters will hate. Harsh words can hit like an iron fist. And they don't always come in the form of a direct insult. "Are you always this happy?" "They act like they never have any problems at home". "I love you but I don't really like your ways". A common auto-response to statements like this might be to internalize the impact and then adjust your behaviors for present company. While modesty has its benefits, there's no real advantage in concealing the joy that comes from something wonderful going on in your life. People who are not genuinely happy for you can say or do things that can cause you to feel like you don't deserve what you have. The fact is, good things happen to people who deserve it and to people who don't deserve it. You can humble down until you're blue in the face, but someone is going to still have a problem with the way you 'carry yourself'. Step back from how it feels and keep loving them right on. Continue to be sincere with yourself and put your energy into preventing your own assumptions about what they're thinking. Find ways to celebrate privately, but don't condemn yourself when your public celebrations cause someone else to feel uncomfortable. Allow God to do the work in them, just as He has done in you.

3. **It's not them, it's you.** Your 'off day' is a problem for others. Do you have the kind of smile that lights up a room? Are you the life of the party? On your worst day when you'd rather stay home with your head buried under the covers, people will expect you to shine as you usually do. If you come into the room and don't smile, someone will inevitably ask you, "What's wrong?" and while you won't feel like explaining there'll be no relief for you until you can be alone again. So while you'd like to show up in your usual places and just be silent, your silence will throw other people completely off balance. It's not fair and there is no real justification for this that will make you feel any better about it. It sucks, but when you're someone who's generally on his A game, people rely on seeing you at your best! Does this mean everyone else is entitled to an off day, except you? Certainly not. But it does mean you that must accept that if you do have an off day, it will impact more than you. Embrace, don't resent, the charge that comes with having the ability to influence. Sure it may be influence you didn't ask for or maybe even don't feel you deserve. But you'll be better off facing the truth, you're a game-changer. Life has a way of reminding us that even our worst issues aren't entirely about us. Is it such a bad thing that someone else can smile more easily because of your presence? Is it a curse that the tone of your voice brings a peace or tranquility to the hearts of other men or women? Honestly, you probably have more good days than bad days. But if a bad day should come, allow yourself the emotional freedom to feel, but rather than act on those feelings, act on God's truth. Perhaps it's just one of those times when you don't need to be around too many people. Don't stay away too long though – there is strength in the fellowship of saints, no matter what they need from you or vice versa.

4. **The higher you go, the tighter the air.** It is a pretty well-known fact that snakes can't survive on airplanes above a

certain altitude. This imagery has been used to illustrate that there are principalities in life who want to steal your joy, kill your hope and destroy your aspirations. Snakes aren't the only ones who don't survive high altitudes. As you ascend to new levels in Christ and the life He has for you, some of your comforts will fall away as you go. Not every bird flies in a flock. A few of the birds in your life won't be able to soar to the heights for which you are destined. Very few people are willing to follow the path that leads to greatness. (Matt 7:13-14) People may see the glory in your life, but they may not see the hardships and effort required that got you to that place. If God is promoting you, it's okay to miss the consolation that companionship offers. It is not okay to allow your longings to hinder you from saying yes to God. Do yourself a favor and seek the comfort from God and the new provisions He is making for you. He'll never take you someplace that hasn't been fully furnished with everything you need to be successful.

5. **You may have to be the bigger person… again.** Stars shine all the time, but they appear brightest when the sky is in the darkest phase of nighttime. They are light years away, yet they appear as brilliant gems on the horizon of a blue-black ocean. With all that shining power, they still don't shine so when it's day. Instead they wait patiently for the sun to set knowing that while they must yield to its superior light all day, their time will come. In this life, conflict will arise. As it does, leaders must also rise to the occasion. It's important to sharpen your conflict management skills if you're going to shine brightly in this world. God gave man dominion over every living creature, except other humans. This means there will be seasons for you to shine, and seasons to simply flicker. It takes spiritual wisdom and discernment to know which time is which. Everyone faces conflict in some form or fashion. The art of submission can be a great ally to

you on such occasions. You are a creature of greatness; this comes with some exclusive obligations. You may have to smile when you don't feel like it. Give when you'd rather not. Show up when you feel like sleeping in. Bow out of the fight when you'd rather blow up the place. You can be surrounded by people who appear to be exempt from the same standards you feel responsible to, and you'll feel like God is unfairly holding you alone to His standard. Suck it up, He is. God desires a more excellent way for those whom He calls to greatness. Sure you forgave ten times before; if it glorifies God you just may have to do it again. Acceptance of God's higher standard shows that you are maturing in your walk. When you can embrace that standard, you will show forth fruits that are too vast to measure and too incredible to believe. Be brilliant, be beautiful, be brazen but allow God to show you when it's time to be abased.

6. **Your meekness will, at times, be mistaken for weakness.** When you're kind to someone whose behavior is hostile, it can look like you're being weak. Taking the higher road and walking away from naysayers doesn't mean you aren't strong or that you're not willing to stand up for yourself. Still, there will be times when the best thing for everyone is for you to stand down in the face of adversity. It's human nature to associate strength with the exertion of power. Intellectually it just makes sense. But God's nature doesn't rely on human intellect. Meekness is a spiritual attribute. It's like a divine muscle that is shaped and strengthened by being worked out. You'll notice it getting stronger by its demonstration in times of adversity. Christians have a different understanding about what it means to demonstrate meekness and it has everything to do with being strong. Rick Warren has often referred to meekness as being, "strength under control. (2 Tim 1:7). As long as you know you CAN respond differently, keep your faith and your responses in check and don't worry

that others can't see it. It's not them you'll have to give an account to on judgment day, but God. Why not handle it in a way that is acceptable to Him?

7. **With great power comes great responsibility.** The same holds true for liberty in Christ by the way. We are the managers or stewards of the time, talent and treasures that God (the Creator and the patent owner) has given us. If you have been given a talent, wouldn't it be irresponsible not to reverence God with its use? If you become wealthy, use your wealth to improve the conditions of life for your loved ones, your church or your community. Don't squander your wealth on temporary gratuities that won't amount to a hill of beans when this world is over. It's an honorable thing to leave an inheritance for loved ones or future generations. How can you do so in a way that brings God glory and encourages others to know Him? Even your beauty can be used to extol The Lord. The most lovely face in the world is only made more beautiful when accompanied by a pure heart. There are so many advantages that come with certain benefits or privileges from God. Like a driver's license opens up access to do things non-drivers cannot, blessings can provide access exclusively for the one being blessed. Power, influence and access unlike before the blessing. That kind of power can be dangerous in the hands of the wrong person. It's your responsibility when God blesses you, to dedicate the gift back to the giver and follow His guidance for what to do with it. Use your powers for good and not evil.

God has given each of you a gift from his great variety of spiritual gifts. Use them well to serve one another. Do you have the gift of speaking? Then speak as though God himself were speaking through you. Do you have the gift of helping others? Do it with all the strength and energy that God supplies. Then everything you do will bring glory to God through Jesus Christ. All glory and power to him forever and ever! Amen. (I Peter 4:10-11)

This kind of truth tends to manifest through painful life situations. It's tough when your good looks initiate snide remarks anytime you're in a crowd. There aren't many support groups for misunderstood wealthy people. Smart kids tend to generally be labeled as underdogs; some even embrace their inner nerd, but it doesn't remove the sting of a disparaging remark at high noon on the school playground. There is enough pressure to perform when you begin to tap into the greatness that God has designed within you. If you don't have a balanced sense of who you are, it can lead to a warped sense of how you see and interact with others. How can you be true to yourself if you haven't really grasped who you are? Take the time to ask God all about you and become as versed in your strengths as you are with your flaws. Make a list and read it aloud until you become comfortable hearing you promote you.

Repent for those thoughts and behaviors which undermined God's plan for your life. He's an amazing God and there are no power outages when it comes to His light! Did you ever try to conceal your blessings or refuse to step out in your faith because you wanted to make sure others didn't think you were high-minded or biggity? In your effort to be seen in a respectable light, you may have destroyed any ability for others to genuinely see God. Some of you know that you're an anointed Usher, but you won't serve on the board because "someone else may want a chance". God doesn't reason as we do. It's Him who gives the anointing and does the appointing, so why wouldn't you serve with excellence and make His heart glad. Are you a good husband who loves and cares for his family but you've stopped being affectionate or playful with them in public because you feel like you're offending the single-parent who is watching? You can probably think of a million little adjustments you've made to safeguard yourself from the misconceptions of the world concerning whatever your blessing is. In doing so, you have been trying to put a basket over a burning flame that will never be able to extinguish the light. Your man-made form of humility cannot match God's which is divine and achieves the grace you're really in need of. You may even be producing a weakened version of those attributes which are intended to glorify God and as a result, people won't be able to see His goodness in your life. The deficient model of a godly but destitute lifestyle was obliterated once Christians understood that holiness and poverty aren't one in the same. Forgive yourself for not knowing this or not seeing how your behaviors promoted this false impression of God, and move on. Stop apologizing for being rich or smart or talented and unleash your true potential to really shine a light in this dark and evil world. You're not in it alone. God is with you and He is faithful to finish the good works that He started when He first chose you. (Phil 1:6) It's time to stop hiding from your blessings.

Once you've forgiven yourself, forgive anyone who has misjudged you. Were you treated unfairly because you have some rights and benefits that others did not? If so, be grateful and not guilty because you know that everything is in God's hands and the same One who gives, can take it away at any moment. Appreciate your special privileges and be a power for good. As much as it hurts, there will be people who aren't pleased to see you soar. Pray for them and try not to kick up too much dust as you lift off.

It's comforting to know you can ask God's Holy Spirit to search your heart in case their misgivings about you happen to be accurate. There are times when pride or greed may creep in and stir us to sinful motives. This is a good place to let the Holy Spirit work in order to get you back on track. It's the responsibility that comes with having the privileges of God. Besides, God's children love correction – we know and appreciate its benefits! Allowing Him to remove any impure thoughts or actions that can affect your love for yourself, God and His people is like taking a laxative in preparation for running a race. You'll be at your leanest and most efficient state when you get rid of any weight that might slow you down. (Heb 12:1) If you can develop this skill, you'll be free from the guilty feelings or maltreatment and anything else that tries to slow down your progress for God. You can freely and humbly enjoy the advantages you have, and you'll even be able to bless others!

It is possible to be your best self with a righteous balance of distinction and amenability. God is the most imaginative being and He has the most elaborate plans for our lives. There's no need to play an uncomfortable game of kowtowing to others out of anxiety about what someone may think. Let God deal with the hearts of man. You can avail yourself with a willing heart, to be the brilliant and most luminous light for God that this world will see. If by your life He is glorified, others will come to know Him just as lovingly as you once did.

> This little light of mine
> I'm gonna let it shine
> Let it shine   Let it shine   Let it shine
> (Harry Dixon Loes, circa 1920)

AFTERWORD

Sorry Not Sorry celebrates favor and issues a challenge to readers, to embrace blessings. By doing so, your light can shine brightly where others will see the love of God and be drawn to Him. Many are called [to serve others with their gifts] but few are chosen [and given favor, benefits and exclusivity]. For those who will answer the Call to greatness, an exceptional experience is promised. It isn't all easy, but for the person who boldly embraces blessings, you can shine brightly in this life without giving up eternity with God in the next life. (Phil 2:6)

The author shares her revelations when a mind-blowing encounter with God rips the cover off of some small yet erroneous thoughts and behaviors in her daily life. She connects a series of personal revelations about why and how we should live with gratitude, not guilt, for the favor that God grants to us. How does it feel when people see your glory but don't know your story? How can you move forward confidently when you're the object of envy? These thoughts and others may leave you feeling as though you don't deserve the goodness around you.

Sorry Not Sorry offers encouragement and strategies for anyone who has lived with guilt because their own unique gifts or advantages brought about a spotlight that wasn't desired. Consider her bold declarations about how many benevolent Christians can dishonor God by playing down the greatness that He places within us. Wealth, beauty, intellect, confidence and even holiness are assets that can be used to bring strength to believers and light to those in darkness. Still, bible doctrine often highlights the slippery slope down which many of these benefits can lead us when pride accompanies those gifts. In response, we may try to manufacture our own self-made brand of humility so others don't think we're being arrogant or high-minded. As well-intentioned as it is, our brand of any virtue can't match God's sincere virtue, so it cannot be effective for His glory.

BIBLIOGRAPHY

Buber, Martin. *I and Thou.* 2nd Ed. New York, NY: Scribner, 1958.

Williamson, Marianne. *A Return to Love: Reflections on the Principles of a Course in Miracles.* New York, NY: HarperCollins, 1992.

About the Author

Angela N. Parris, writes with an incurable appetite for displaying the love *and* life that God designed for his people. Untethered, she conveys the wisdom and transparency of a young disciple - or one who knows just enough to be wise, but not enough to be Master. Parris inspires readers to hunger for righteousness, so that they may personally know and share the immeasurable depth of Christ's love with the world around them.

The absence of earthly credentials never stopped her star from shining. She has worked *as* and *for* executive, political and spiritual leadership throughout her lifetime and just after age 40, Parris decided to move out in the one gift she has been praised for since childhood - writing.

Born in California and raised on the East Coast, she now lives in Upstate New York and serves faithfully in ministry with her husband Carl, their six children, a singing dog named Miss Melody, two cool cats Kasper and Mercedes and a turtle, name unknown.

Printed in the United States
by Baker & Taylor Publisher Services